HEY KID

LETTERS FROM A DAD

BY
ALAN PACKER

DAWN PACKER, EDITOR

Integrity House
Blowing Rock, NC

Published by

Integrity House

A Publishing Company
P.O. Box 2108
Blowing Rock, NC 28605
1-800-915-1333

Library of Congress
#99-094564

Printed in United States of America

Cover Design by Dana Willett

For Laura, my wife,
I could not have done it
without you.

In memory of all the actual
and potential fathers
who lost their lives in Vietnam.

Acknowledgements

I want to deeply thank the following people:

First and foremost, my daughter, Dawn, for never breaking off our ability to communicate and permitting me to share these letters with others.

Lila McGinnis, author, teacher and friend, who made me act on my dream of writing.

Jerry Burns, editor, and Bill Cummins, publisher, of **The Blowing Rocket**, *who believed in me enough to print these letters as a column in their newspaper.*

Dana Willett, a wonderful graphic artist, who led me through the technical maze of layout and design.

Most importantly, to my wife, Laura, for being with me as mother to my daughter. Your input gave Dawn wonderful dimensions that I could have never provided.

HEY KID

Contents

Introduction

While my daughter was in high school, several parents approached me to ask, "Why is Dawn so different than my child?" They wondered how she and I had maintained such a close relationship through the "rough teen years." I didn't know how to respond at that time, but their questions forced me to examine the interaction between Dawn and me.

I think the key to our relationship was actually very simple. It started when Dawn was about two years old. I saw that she was a very unique individual, not just a "child". She was not a puppet whose strings I could pull nor a piece of clay that I could mold to my specifications. I realized that I had to interact and communicate with this little person as I would with any adult. Her needs were not my needs, her talents were not my talents, our personalities were not the same. The simplicity of my approach was just respect for who Dawn was and I spoke to her with that attitude.

This book of letters is part of that process. These are letters that I wrote to Dawn while she was in college. They cover many subjects — some practical, some philosophical. Several are simply written summaries of conversations between us. I also shared some of the approaches I used while raising her, so that she would know why I treated her

11

the way I did.

I think it is the responsibility of parents to state our values and the reasoning behind them. I think it is important to say lying is wrong because I know the consequences of lying. If I do not teach my child these things, who will? These letters were a way to restate the hard learned lessons of my life. Whether our children accept or reject our values is not the issue.

Dawn extended me a great compliment by believing I had something to share with others and that these letters were the best way to do it. Our first printing has yielded some wonderful results. I have received letters and e-mails and had parents track me down to tell me this book helped them broach subjects they had previously avoided. A Vietnam Veteran was finally able to talk to his adult children about the war. One father has read a letter a night to his children as a discussion starter.

This book is about communication which is the key to good relationships with our children, as with others in our lives. The relationship between a parent and child should be one of life's greatest treasures for each of us.

13   HEY KID

Reading for Life

Hey Kid,

A full scholarship to college! Let me again say how proud I am of you. When you started your freshman year of high school, I said that you had to do your part and Mom and I would do ours to get you through college. You did your part excellently: your high grades, your hours of outside writing, the jobs you worked. To get a full ride based on your writing skills is a real accomplishment.

I believe those skills started when you were an infant and Mom would hold you in her lap with a book and point and laugh and talk to you. She made books so much fun even before you could talk. She insisted we read to you often and always before bed. Books were a major part of our family life.

Since I always had a book handy and read tons, it was a perfect way for me to spend time with you because I wasn't sure what to do with a little person. If a book got torn, you and I would tape it up together very seriously because "books were important." As you grew older, we spent hours and hours reading together in the front room. We had great times sharing funny or interesting things from our books. Many discussions on values and morals came up from those reading sessions.

Mom also taught me about the importance of having you read out loud. Your verbal skills were always high, and I think reading aloud was a big part of that. It was another way to spend time together and share. We also could hear whether you were pronouncing words right and detect any problems like dyslexia that may have needed help.

I had my own suggestions also. I had you read a biography each week in late grade school. Not only did it expose you to non-fiction, but it provided many examples of how people lived and thought and achieved their goals. Even the infamous people had something to teach you and gave us more opportunities to discuss right and wrong and what is important in life.

I also tried to talk about books to other people in front of you, so you could see their interest and excitement about learning new things. I knew that books could give you an education then and for the rest of your life.

The one place Mom would not let us read was at the table during meals. At first I resented that because I had always used meal time to consume books. But she was right. We talked about many things at the table. We shared work, school, money problems, successes, and failures — and what we had read about.

Keep up the good work, and let me know which books you read in college that I should grab. We can still share in spite of the distance.

Love, Dad

Why I Went to Vietnam

Hey Kid,

I was really touched that you chose to take a history course on Vietnam. I know how much that war affected your life as I tried to work through all the rage and survival guilt I brought home with me. Despite the negative consequences of that period of my life, I am still proud I served and want you to know why I went to Vietnam.

I was born during World War II and grew up with relatives and neighbors who had fought to keep Europe free from the Nazis. Our country was still in a "cold war" against Communism. It became apparent to me that freedom was tremendously important and worth any price to keep. What would life be worth if you could not choose what you wanted to do with it? How could you raise children if they had no hope of becoming the people they were capable of being? I loved the excitement of having a choice in everything about my life. We are so fortunate to live in a country that permits this. But as they say, "Freedom is not free."

Someone has to stand up to the oppressor. The policeman on the beat, the bystander who steps in on a mugging, and the soldier who faces an organized army — each helps someone to stay free from oppression. In our country, most of these people

17

are just everyday people who are suddenly placed in a very dangerous situation. They are not Rambos. They are scared to death, but they still do their jobs to maintain freedom — their own and that of others.

The Vietnamese people are just like us. They have families, hopes and dreams. All they want is to be free to live their lives. I went there to help them do that. Most of the men I served with went with the same idea. This is what we do as Americans. We did not know the international politics. I still do not understand the tremendous protests against helping someone try to stay free. I often wonder if it was because they were South Asians, not our cultural ancestors. Would the protest have been there if it was a European country? Were the Vietnamese not worth fighting for?

Am I kidding myself about all of this? I don't know, but after 30 years away from Vietnam, I still feel we let those people down. I still mourn the boat people who died in the South China Sea trying to flee the Communists. They faced death with their families rather than living under oppression. They just wanted what we have — freedom.

Please, do not ever take your freedom lightly. Your choice of education, where to live, who you associate with are all part of that. You do not live in fear of being hauled off in the middle of the night because you don't agree with the government. Freedom affects everyday life in endless ways, but we tend to forget that.

I love my freedom and the life it has given me. I think everyone should live like this. So that is why, even though I was scared to death and didn't want to fight a war, I went to Vietnam.

Love, Dad

5'6" Professional Basketball Player

Hey Kid,

It's always so great to receive one of your letters. Your observations about your college friends were interesting, and I'm glad that you are so comfortable with them.

The most interesting statement you made was, "Some of my friends do not know that they can change who they are. I have areas in my life that I still don't like, but I know I can change those." I am so thankful to hear that from you. I am not sure what areas concern you, but they are not as important as your realization that you can make true changes in attitudes and self-worth.

I think your confidence in this area comes from the fact that Mom and I never tried to hide our weaknesses from you and openly let you see many of the struggles it took to change. I vowed I would not be a "Superman" father who never let his child see his human side. Children who grow up with that type of parent never feel they are as good as they should be.

Let me share some of the things that are important when you look at your own life. First, never compare yourself to other people. It is okay to admire others and their talents, but you are not them. Can you imagine me wanting to be a professional basketball player at five foot six inches? I have to be realistic. We must look at what we "bring to the table" and enjoy ourselves, not what the other person brings.

Secondly, work hard at deciding what you believe about life and then live by it. Is truth important? Are friends important? Is knowledge more important than material things? Is it wrong to be fake or are there times for it? You have to make many decisions about your values and then consistently live that way. When you waver, you become very uncomfortable with yourself. It is better to choose a belief, live by it, and find out you are wrong than not to live by any set values.

Third, and maybe most important, is to look at your mistakes and forgive yourself for them. Look at my life. It was so crazy and wild that I constantly messed things up. I cannot change one bit of my past. I can be sorry and try to make amends, but the best thing I can do is forgive myself and try to be a better man now and in the future.

If I do not forgive myself, I will stay in the past because I will not feel good about the positive things I am doing now. Today I walk around proud that I have truly changed my lifestyle. I don't care what people know about my past. No matter what they know, they have the reality of my life now. I could not feel this positive if I had not finally forgiven myself.

Keep looking at your life. Keep working on it. But most importantly, keep being you.

Love, Dad

Snobs

Hey Kid,

Remember those four rich women who walked through our store last summer with their noses so high they were oxygen starved? They had spent more money on their clothes than we did for our car. We laughed when they left and wondered why people acted like that just because they had money. Since then I have seen many obviously wealthy people come through this store. Some were like those women and others were just nice. What is the difference? I think it may be a matter of how they value themselves.

I think snobs don't have any inner value and thus cling to outward shows of money, intellectualism, or who they know. Because they feel they have nothing to offer, they have to create superiority. I feel sorry for them because surely they have some neat things without depending on what money can buy for them. I also wonder what would happen if one of them went broke. Would the others still be her friends?

Snobs must also exclude from their lives many truly wonderful people who are not wealthy. That can go the other way also. But just take us as an example. They walked by a father and daughter who are very good friends and enjoy doing stuff together. We create, are helpful to others, don't cheat people, laugh a bunch, and a lot of other things that many people would envy. The snobs will never know us, and I think that is their loss. Does this sound snobbish from my side? I hope not. There are so many wonderful people in this world that it is crazy to snub them.

When you were in grade school and pulled down some good grades on your report card, we had a talk about pride. Remember? I told you that if I ever saw you brag or get cocky about your grades, I would kick your little butt. I said you were only one chromosome away from Special Olympics and that you personally had nothing to do with that. Rather than being proud of our minds, we should wake up every day and be thankful for the gift. (The kick in the butt still goes.)

I'm proud that you see so much good in others most of the time. I know it can be hard. The way I do it is to look at all the negatives in myself. Then other people start looking a whole lot better.

Just remember, snobbishness comes in many forms and sometimes it is very subtle — like being an editor on the college paper and researching only one side of a problem.

Of course, knowing I have the greatest kid in world isn't being snobbish. It's just the truth.

Love, Dad

Nose Rings

Hey Kid,

Eric, my best man on the roofing crew, showed up on the job with a nose ring! I already worked through his unusual hair and pierced ears, but a nose ring?

I am generally very accepting of people and their quirks, but I am so protective of the great image my little company has that I overreacted at first. I couldn't laugh when he said he wouldn't wear it every day because he had several other ones to wear.

Young people who wear wild hairdos and nose or tongue rings often complain because they can't get some jobs. Hey, that's life. I could not be a banker or doctor the way I look. If you choose to be different, you must be willing to accept the limitations that come with that. Is it worth it? Only each person can decide for himself. To me there is no cost because I am who I want to be. I am willing to forego certain occupations and acquaintances.

I believe part of my reaction to Eric's nose ring was that conservative, proper business training I had received in the '60s. I was taught that people did not want to deal with those who looked or acted "differently" than the normal businessman. This is from me, the guy who never looks normal except at funerals.

Part of that old training is still valid. First impressions are extremely important. To you, it may seem that your dad never worried about that in his life. I did, but before you were old enough to understand. By the time you realized I had my own business, sold my own jobs, and generally dealt with an upper income-level customer, I was well-established and running on my reputation. People sought me out and were often surprised at the strange-looking man who showed up at their door. But their first impression came from whoever told them about my craftsmanship.

I am sure I lost some jobs because of my appearance. That was, and still is, a price I am willing to pay. I just refuse to be what some people want me to be. I can't keep up with all the needs people have. I work as much as I want and my customers trust me. That is what counts to me, not having everyone think I'm wonderful or the perfect looking businessman.

So I went to work looking at the reality of the situation. Eric was not the first impression our customers had of our company. They had already signed a contract before he showed up on the job. Eric was a really hard worker who was liked by all my customers because of his humor and straightforward answers to their questions. His sincerity was real, and he would do anything to make sure the job went correctly. I knew the nose ring would not change this. It was my problem, not his.

Love, Dad

Respect at Two

Hey Kid,

Stopped to see our friends with the two-year-old daughter, Cindy. We played, Cindy and I. It was so much fun. She is such an interesting little lady. Her mom is reading to her a lot, talks to her as a person, and involves her in many of the everyday little things that teach skills. It is so great to see that kind of interaction between a parent and child.

Then her mother and I tried to talk about writing. Immediately Cindy had to show her mother something that was down in the basement. The mother asked her to wait a minute, but Cindy started to whine and insist that her mother come with her. The mother did. When she got back, she looked at me and shrugged her shoulders like "What can you do?" Since she and I are good friends and have had other child-raising talks, I told her.

I said the real issue here was respecting other people. The mother raised her eyebrows in surprise, obviously not expecting this to be the point of discussion. Cindy is old enough to start learning to respect other people's time. This is not a teen issue — by then it is too late. I used to tell you that I would be with you in five minutes; until then, it was my time to talk to whomever. Then I made sure I was back to you in five minutes.

This taught you that other people had a right to share your father's time, but that you were still important because I did return my attention to you when I said I would.

The mother had just taught Cindy that neither her time or mine was important when she gave in and went to the basement. There is no magic moment in a child's life when he or she becomes respectful of other people. It has to be taught and it has to start very early. There are many heartbroken parents who do not understand why their teenage children are so disrespectful. These people did not realize that it was their job to actively teach respect, starting at a very early age.

To me, it was always such a reward to see your eyes when my attention came back to you. You knew then that I had not just put you off and that you were important. Your self-concept was better by learning respect. You would not have felt good about yourself by only getting your way through whining.

Why do parents not see this? For one thing, it seems ("seems" is the essential word here) easier to just give in. This may be true in the short term, but living with a whining child cannot really be better than standing up to her a few times.

Teach your children respect for others. They will respect you because they cannot manipulate you, and they will feel better about themselves. This is lifetime lesson, not a one time deal.

Love, Dad

Academics vs. Education

Hey Kid,

Now that you are all settled into your college life I want to share some of my thoughts on academics. I have many mixed emotions on the value of a college education.

When I was in college there were good professors and bad ones. Such is life in all fields. Some of these people think they are gods and seem to enjoy running over the top of students to show their intellectual superiority. Do not let these professors intimidate you. You are there for your education, not their selfish needs. If you can still learn what you want to learn from them, stay in the class. If the only benefit of staying is earning credit hours, drop it and get into a class that will educate you.

You have to remember that much of the academic world is set up to perpetuate itself, not to prepare you for the world. Academics only respect degrees. You need a PhD to teach upper level courses. You can only get a PhD if you research and write in a prescribed manner. They stick to their rigid formats and refuse to accept thousands of experienced and self-educated people who could offer you a meaningful education.

You must have high grades to get into graduate school. You only need to get into graduate school to be an academic or work in one of the professions that require higher degrees. Out in life your grade point average doesn't mean anything, but your education (and how you use it) does. My father did not have a formal education, but many times I saw engineers come to him to help design heating and ventilation systems that were too sophisticated for them. Dad could do it because of his experience and self-education. He loved to teach others, but never would have been accepted by the academics because he "only" had a high school education.

Don't get me wrong, there are some wonderful educators out there. I had an English history professor who enthralled and excited me with the flow and interaction of history. To this day I love to read historical books and am able to see my life within the context of history because of him.

I took a graduate course on small group communications because I was doing public speaking and leading several different workshops. I had hoped to improve my skills. The class was all theory: "If X group acts this way, how will Y group respond?" I asked my prof if we were going to actually get into real group situations and practice skills. He said, "No, and I probably could not help you if we did. You have more speaking experience in front of real audiences than I do." Much of the department was like that. All theory, no experience. I left graduate school and have never regretted it. I learned more by actually doing things than those classes could teach me in the time I would have spent in them.

Get "your" education in college, not someone else's interpretation of it. Expose yourself to all the new ideas you can and then you can decide if this information is valuable to you. Remember, you must educate yourself; no one else can.

Love, Dad

Over the Edge

Hey Kid,

These mountains are so beautiful. When I see certain cliffs, I regret that I have not yet taught you to rappel. When you were young I loaned my equipment to a "friend." He left town and I never saw the gear again. For years we could not afford to buy new stuff and, now that we can, you are not here. We still will do it some day because it is really fun and has other benefits.

I have taught dozens of people to rappel down cliffs. Most of them were terrified at the thought of leaning back over a three or four-story drop and trusting that equipment with their lives. Some literally moaned in fear or cried. I would gently, but firmly, talk them over the edge. When they touched bottom, they were always thrilled that they had done it. They were never the same once they had faced that fear and conquered it. They found out they could still do things in spite of their fear. That is what I was really teaching them, not rappelling.

I taught two brothers, ages eight and ten, along with their mother to rappel. When we faced a seventy-foot cliff, the older boy would not do it. The eight-year-old did. The mother told me later that the older boy had always bullied and dominated the younger. After the rappelling experience, when the older boy would try to pick on his brother, the younger one just said,

"Get off my case. You couldn't even face the cliff." That young man learned about himself on that rope.

It is important to take people beyond the normal. Going to a professional football game is fun, but it does not affect your life much. I always tried to offer experiences to people that would also teach them about themselves. A girl in one of my youth groups wanted to parachute jump and her father would not go with her. She asked me if I would take her. I said I would if I could find another adult to go with us. We did it and she was thankful and felt good about herself. She had gone way beyond the normal. Several years later her father thanked me for taking her and said he really regretted not having done it with her. He said he missed a tremendous growth experience with his daughter.

When I trained people in rescue work, my students had to lower me down off a building while strapped helplessly in a rescue basket for the final test. One mistake and I could literally die. They knew that was coming from day one and the effect was electrifying to most of them. It was no longer simply learning knots and pulleys. It was responsibility for my life. When I climbed out of that basket on the ground, they danced with relief and pride. They really did it. It wasn't just another test.

Try to give people the gift of experience that includes personal growth. It means so much more than material things.

Love, Dad

There May Be No Tomorrows

Hey Kid,

Don't faint — another letter so soon. Actually, Mom let me read your letter to her and it made me want to comment on part of it.

You said, "My problem wasn't gleaning support for what I wanted, it was finding something to want — and still is." I think this may be my fault in some ways. My goals probably were not apparent to you. Most of your life you saw me in a struggle for survival as opposed to attaining planned goals. Prior to your birth my goals were never tangible; they were more for risk and danger or the "forbidden." Only in these last few years have I actually started to form specific goals. So you never did get much of an example from me as to setting positive goals and attaining them.

Also, my lack of caring about material things or what other people think had to have a major effect on you. Many people who are extremely driven are thus because of their need for approval. You and I tend to need approval only from a very small, select group in our lives.

I think it is hard to say that integrity and friends are goals. They are important motivators, but may not seem like real desires. We do not sit down and say, "I will attain seven great friends in my life." Likewise, integrity cannot be quantified and is not considered a measurable goal. But these things are what will count at the end of the road. I hope you will be proud of me for being a man of integrity and a true friend to those around me.

One tremendous influence on me (and thus on how I taught you to look at life) was my Vietnam experience. I never saw life the same way after that. I am still so thankful that I lived to be a father and do all the other wonderful things I have done. That war made me appreciate each little thing and each day.

I am sure this sounds like "eat, drink, and be merry," but after that war it was hard to plan anything because I realized how mortal I was. There may be no tomorrows. Today is what is important. So long term goals were not a high priority in my life. Enjoying you and Mom each day was far more important than retirement money or future admiration from others.

Do not get frustrated about your search for what to do with your life. Do whatever you do with integrity and care for those who are important in your life. Then, whatever you do, I believe you will find it fulfilling.

This may not sound like a lot of help, but believe me — it is very important that you understand this first.

Love, Dad

Credit is Like Crystal

Hey Kid,

So the credit card blitz has started? Those banks aren't dumb. They know that, if they can get you using a credit card the first year in college, they will probably keep you using it. Just make sure you use it wisely or it will be using you.

My father used to tell me that your credit rating was like fine crystal — one crack and it was ruined. I never forgot that and have always protected my credit rating, even at great personal sacrifice. That attitude has really paid off for us as a family.

When I went to college, my dad co-signed a $1000 note with the local bank for me. I was eighteen and paid it back within a year. Ever since then I have been able to walk into that bank and borrow money for my business. When I married your mom, the bank financed our first truck for the roofing business. After two years I wanted to buy a very expensive piece of equipment, but had not built up enough equity for them to loan me that much money. Because of my credit record with them, they offered to buy the equipment and lease it to me. That machine jumped us into a five state business and we never looked back. It was all due to my track record of never missing a payment.

Credit is critical to make it on your own when you don't have anything but integrity. If you want to build your own business, buy a house, or be able to get money for emergencies, start now to establish your credit history as someone who *always* pays on time.

It feels good to have people totally trust your word when it comes to paying your bills. I can walk into any supplier I have ever dealt with and get products just by saying, "I'll send you a check when I get home." Recently I bought several hundred dollars worth of product from a supplier I have not dealt with in three years and which is 500 miles away from me now. I asked if I could send a check the next week and they said yes. They did not even ask for my current address. That is a nice way to live.

When I got sick and lost my ability to do business for a year and a half, we got pretty desperate. I finally went to a business friend and told him I needed $10,000 to start over. He wrote me a check without even blinking. He trusted me to pay him back and knew I would help him any way I could if he needed it.

Sometimes it is very good business to use credit. Handle it with care lest you crack it.

Love, Dad

Coffee in Russia

Hey Kid,

I'm getting the old travel bug again as I write to my friends in Europe. Can't hardly stand to read the "National Geographic"— it just makes me want to pack my bag and go.

There are so many neat people in this world that I wonder who I am missing. I enjoy the sightseeing attractions and museums, but it's the people I meet who make my travels so great. Mom wonders how I could spend two weeks in a country and come back with only six pictures. All were pictures of people sitting around a table someplace in France, Finland, or Russia. Each was special to me.

It is the sharing of lifestyles and thoughts that is wonderful to me. I have "broken bread" with people in Paris, Papua New Guinea, Finnish Lapland, Russia, Southern France, Helsinki, and Vietnam. The food was different, but the people weren't.

The most memorable event for me was in St. Petersburg, Russia. Remember, the Russians had been the enemy for all of my life and I had been their enemy. I was born during World War II and grew up during the Cold War. I had men killed by Russian weapons in Vietnam.

A group of us had gone to the St. Petersburg symphony. Afterward, we went to a coffee bar and talked for almost three hours. There were two Russian women, one Russian man, a British couple, a lady from Finland, and me. We covered many topics, but the biggest ones were Vietnam and Afghanistan. Since I had served in Vietnam and the Russians knew young men who had served in Afghanistan, we found common ground in our opinions of war and freedom and the price that we must pay for it.

The Russians at this table had lived under Communism and were now experiencing their first taste of freedom. It was great to sit together and talk as people who had hopes and dreams and families we loved. It was healing for me to see Russians as everyday people even though I academically already knew it. It was good to know they hated war and wanted freedom as much as the Finns, Brits, and Americans. They worried about their parents and children. Their daily lives were just like mine, only with fewer choices. I will never forget that evening. I gained compassion for millions of people who I had always disliked because they were theoretically my enemy.

I love to meet other people and experience their cultures. It may be the best way to eliminate prejudice. You cannot break bread with someone and consider them to be your enemy or lower than you. We need to do this in our own country also. If you truly listen, you will learn that they are us and we are them.

Love, Dad

Moving into Action

Hey Kid,

I said I'd get back to you on goal setting, so here we go. Goal setting is one of those things everyone talks about, but few people do (or at least do very well). Of course you can have more than one goal in life at a time, but there are generally some that are more important or more dominant at any given time.

The reason many of our goals are not realized is that we do not make them specific enough. I can say that I want to be a writer. A good goal? Yes. But it is not specific enough. I need to ask myself: fiction or non-fiction? adult or children? historical or contemporary? realistic or fantasy? I could go on and on. Until I decide on a specific type of writing, I will probably not accomplish anything. Once I decide exactly what type of writing I want to do, I will have a definite course of action to follow.

I will have to determine the language level of my readers. I will have to choose a subject that is new or presented from a different slant. I will have to find publishers that print that type of writing. I will (don't laugh) actually have to start writing. Specific goals give you something to do; general goals do not.

Goal setting moves you to action and should make you use your time more efficiently. If you don't know what to do, just ask yourself, "What am I doing today to reach my goal?" If it is a motivating goal, you will make choices between goofing off or doing something valuable. For me it may mean the difference in what I read for that day. Do I read this great fiction book I have or do I research other books for my own novel? Specific goals determine how you use your time.

Big goals are generally just a bunch of little goals. Once you decide on your main goal, you simply make a list of all the obstacles that will keep you from accomplishing it. I know this sounds negative, but I like thinking like this because then I have something to conquer. Each of these obstacles becomes a mini-goal and gives you one or more specific things to do—like going to the library to find out who publishes children's books and who wants your exact type of book. Again, big goals simply become a bunch of little goals. This makes you realize you can do big things because they are really just a bunch of little things.

Don't be afraid to change your goal. You may spend a year on a project and find out it is not for you. The key is that you found out. If you never set the specific goal and start to work toward it, you'll never know.

So pick something specific, break it down into all the little parts, and work each day on those little obstacles to your goal. If you know where you want to be five years from now, you have to ask yourself every day, "What am I doing today to get there?"

Love, Dad

Your Violent Dad

Hey Kid,

Do you remember when you were in grade school and someone told you that your daddy was a violent man? You came to me and asked me if I was violent. I said, "Have you ever seen me act violently?" You said that you had not. Then I told you to believe what you see, not what someone tells you.

I think it is time to expand that answer. I probably should have then, but was still afraid of the crazy-Vietnam-Vet label. I realize now that you could have handled the answer and I apologize for not having enough faith in your understanding. The real answer should have been, "I am not a violent man, but I am a man capable of violence."

I think there is a major difference between the two. I am not a violent man because I hate violence and never seek it as an answer to problems. That is the father you saw all your life. I will not even hunt animals because I never want to kill again. I fear any type of violent confrontation. It is a real deep gut fear, the kind that can bring a cold sweat.

How does this fit with a man who is "capable of violence"? When I was trained as an infantryman, we were taught to react with extreme force and violence when our lives were threatened. Soldiers are not trained like policemen who use deadly force only as a last resort. When I got to Vietnam I found out how capable I was of inflicting violence even when I was terrified. I have known ever since that I could do so if the need arose. If anyone would put you or your mom in a life-threatening situation, I know what I am capable of doing. I would be a man you have never seen. Am I proud of this? No, but I am honestly glad I have that information available.

There are those who say all violence is evil and thus I am evil. I agree that violence is wrong, but as long as there are people who willingly do violence, there must be people who can respond. I have asked those purists, "Would you abolish all the police departments right now?" They always say no. They know that they would be victimized quickly without that protection. I am not a self-appointed protector of society and do not believe in vigilantes. Still, I would immediately try to stop, by any means necessary, a person attacking our elderly neighbor if I thought her life was in danger. You can judge your dad based on your experience. I really don't care what the others think of me.

Got pretty heavy here, but life is not all fun and games. I'll be interested in your reaction to all this stuff.

Love, Dad

He's a Liar

Hey Kid,

It happened again. A guy came in the store and asked if we gave decorators a discount. I said that we did not. As he looked around, Mom and his wife started talking. His wife mentioned that her husband was some kind of insurance broker. She laughed and said, "Well, he buys most of the decorations for the house, so I guess he is a decorator." The man lied to save money! They would sell their integrity for 10 percent off!

Every time they come in the store I remember that the guy is a liar. I would never buy insurance from him and have no desire to make friends with him. What a price he paid in respect. How can someone feel good about himself when he has no integrity?

Integrity is one of the hardest things to maintain in my life, but I also think it brings the greatest rewards when achieved. A few years ago I was reroofing a house with 25 year shingles. We ran out of shingles when we were putting on the last caps. We were in a small town and the only shingles that were available in that brand were 20 year shingles. My customer would not know the difference, but I had sold him a 25 year roof. I drove for two hours to buy one bundle of 25 year shingles while my men sat and waited for me. (Of course I paid them for that time. It was not their fault, and they were riding home in a company truck.) After we finished the job and were heading home, one of my men said he could not believe I spent the time and money to do that. That is a normal reaction to integrity, and that is sad. The other man said he was really proud to work for a company with that attitude because he knew we would never cheat anyone. It felt so good to hear that. He will never forget how great it feels to be honest. That was my reward.

When you try very hard to live a life of integrity, the people around you learn this about you. Then they trust you, and I think having someone's trust is wonderful. They share things with you because they know you would never betray them, and they help you because they know you would not take advantage of them. They don't hold mistakes against you because they know you would never intentionally lie to them or do something manipulative to get something for yourself. You don't have to be perfect for people to respect you.

Take integrity into all your relationships whether they be with friends, a spouse, children, boss, employees, or customers. Many times others will not respect it, but that's okay. They are always touched by it whether they acknowledge it or not. Most of all, you will be touched by it. You walk with your head higher, and you will have a confidence in your life that smooths many of the bumps.

Can you imagine what it would do to our relationship if we did not trust each other?

Love, Dad

Fear is Good

Hey Kid,

Thanks for the quick answer to my letter. Your disbelief at my depth of fear in dangerous situations surprises me. I always tried to teach you it was okay to be afraid as long as your fear does not control you. Sometimes I forget that until you experience something, you won't really learn what I am trying to teach. All I can do is warn you or prepare you for those situations. Fear, especially intense fear, is one of them.

Fear is good. Don't ever feel inferior because you feel it. Fear keeps you alive. When I was in Vietnam or working on roofs, the constant recognition that one wrong move could hurt or kill me is one reason I am still here. (The other is grace; sometimes that's the only thing that saves you.) So rather than hating fear, use it. It heightens your senses and quickens your reactions. It is your friend.

Overwhelming fear is not your friend. It is called panic, and panic can get you killed. When I took Lifesaving, my instructor emphasized this point by talking about cramps while swimming. He said anyone can still swim with a cramp. The belief that they cannot causes people to drown. They panic and quit doing what it takes to save themselves. I never forgot that.

The best way to avoid panic is preparation. If someone has a heart attack in front of you, especially if you know them, it is very easy to panic. If you have CPR training, you will still be afraid, but you can do something about it. The work involved keeps panic at bay and limits it to healthy fear. You can save a life while in fear, but not when in panic.

Prepare yourself, mentally and with skills. Don't go water skiing with drunks. Research a foreign country before you go there. There are many ways to minimize fear, but you should never try to totally eliminate it.

When I say I have been in gut wrenching fear, do not be surprised. I almost always had some training to help me deal with the situation. My true panic may come yet, but I keep trying to be ready for the unusual. The best way is to avoid the situation in the first place. With what I know I would not try, for instance, to white-water raft the Colorado by myself, even though I have done several other rivers. Either train or avoid. The key is to not let fear get out of control.

There are times not to show fear. This may be why you were surprised at the depth of my own, even though we have been in some tight spots together. This is not a macho issue, but a leadership issue. If you can appear calm, it will help those around you who may not be prepared to stay steady. Panicking bystanders can be extremely disruptive, and even dangerous. Also, the predator-type person feeds on the fear of others. They really don't want to deal with strength. I have gotten myself out of many situations by simply not displaying the fear I felt. Learn to control your fear and not show it. Preparation is still the best way for both of these.

Love, Dad

Don't Baby-Talk My Kid

Hey Kid,

Congrats on the summer job babysitting. Since you are going to live with them, does that make you a nanny? Three children that young ought to keep you out of trouble.

Since I know you want to make some kind of impact on these kids, I want to share some thoughts with you about children. I know we have touched on some of these before, and you will recognize most from the way you were treated. I just want to formalize them because of your desire to positively touch these children's lives.

My approach to children of any age is that they are simply small, inexperienced people. When you see them this way you cannot treat them the way many people do. For instance, I never baby-talked you and would not let anyone else. Baby-talk assumes that the child's mind does not function as an adult's, and it teaches a lesson that has to be retaught later. Even worse, however, is the lack of respect for that child as a person. I always tried to talk to you as I would any person based on their level of experience. I think this instills a sense of value in the child. They know they are important to you and that what you say to them is valuable. This can be serious or just fun, but the result is the same. They know they are not just some dumb kid. Children may be ignorant, but they are not stupid.

You were just two years old when you asked me if I was angry or frustrated. When I asked if you knew the difference, you said you thought so. I told you I was frustrated, and you said, "Okay" and walked away. People are never surprised when a two-year-old says "elephant," but they are if that same child uses big "adult" words. I think a child attains her vocabulary and knowledge based on how she is spoken to and respected as an intelligent person. That little mind works as well as an adult mind — it just needs to be treated that way.

Children also have a high recognition of integrity and truth within their limited world. When I was very young, I wondered how my mother found out about a broken lamp. She said a little birdy told her. I remember getting really angry because I knew she was lying to me about that bird. She would never say that to Dad, and I knew it. We have to deal with children with as much integrity as we do adults, and maybe even more because they are so honest at that point. It is we adults that teach them to be deceitful by how we act and speak to them.

If you take their emotions seriously, you will deal with their problems seriously. The result is that they will trust you. As a parent you will need this trust to help them when they hit the bigger problems in adolescence and beyond. Trust does not develop automatically between parent and child. I know you are only going to be with these children for one summer, but it is still critical that they feel these things from you.

Love, Dad

Get Out There and Fail

Hey Kid,

Blew it again! I ventured into a business with little experience and didn't have enough capital to make it through all the mistakes. It was quite a learning experience. As my father used to say, "You pay for your education one way or another. You can go to formal school or go to the school of hard knocks." The most important thing here is that I don't quit trying new things.

If I view myself as a failure over this, I could get depressed and want to crawl into a hole. Other people may look at me as a failure, but I can't accept that. I choose to view it as a learning experience that makes me better prepared for the next venture in life. Failing is simply another experience to grow from. Failure is a destructive attitude.

When you have children, let them see you fail at things once in a while. Too many children grow up thinking their parents never mess up or make mistakes. Then they feel like failures when they aren't as "perfect" as Mom and Dad. They do not learn that everyone grows by trying, making mistakes, and trying again. They often quit after one attempt at a project. Imagine believing that good writers only write one draft and then get accepted by the first publisher who sees it. No one is that good, but that is what I used to believe. So I did not even try to write. Now I know better. Don't be afraid to try something because you may not be perfect at it.

Years ago I complained to my friend, Jan, that a youth program I had started was not growing very fast. Jan jumped up and yelled at me, "Stop thinking you are a screwup because your program doesn't have a thousand kids in it! You have done more for those ten kids than anyone else!" I never forgot that. He did me a tremendous favor by pointing out my success, not my self-perceived failing. Since then, I have always tried to be thankful for each positive thing I have done.

I once read a definition of success by Paul Meyer, who founded Success Motivation Institute: "Success is the progressive realization of a worthwhile, predetermined, personal goal." I think it is the best definition of success I have ever read. The key words are "progressive realization." Success is not finally getting to the goal, but the movement, step by step, towards it. Every day that I work at my writing or other goals makes me successful that day. Even making mistakes and correcting them moves me successfully toward my goals.

So all I really have to say to you is "Get out there and keep failing!" That means at least you're getting somewhere and not sitting around afraid to try new things.

Love, Dad

Classes for the Real World

Hey Kid,

The sub-lease you called about brings to mind all those little legal details that come with being on your own. There are so many things that a young person does not have to deal with because Mom and Dad always did. Suddenly those things enter your life in a rush because you are on your own or hitting the age of legal adulthood.

There are several things you can do now to greatly reduce future problems and stresses. You may laugh at some of these, but not for long. The first suggestion, which would apply to your sub-lease questions, is to take a basic business law course.

In this society, where a handshake is no longer enough, you can prevent many problems with this knowledge. It can help with leasing and buying things, car accidents, starting a business or even a marriage. My one law course saved me over a thousand dollars within six months after graduating from college. I was better prepared to deal with a claims adjuster when a lady hit my car. It has saved me thousands since because it taught me the basic premises of the law.

Another course along this line is introductory accounting, not book keeping. The basic concepts of debit/credit, cost accounting, and money controls can affect your approach to your personal budget. They can affect how you buy major items, plan for the future, and listen to the bull salesmen try to feed you. It can take the mystery out of your bank and financial statements too.

Also available are many very pragmatic courses such as basic car care and how your car works. These may help you from getting ripped off on service and prevent many situations that could leave you stranded along the road. It would also show you how to extend the life of your vehicle which is worth thousands in future costs. I have always kept my vehicles for over 150,000 miles and you know my favorite van made it 360,000 miles with no major repairs.

I took a carpentry course once. I didn't want to be a carpenter, but the $200 I spent for the course will save me money and headaches if I ever have a home built. It has already saved me many problems installing items around the house because I understand the basics of framing.

The final suggestion is not really a specific thing, but an attitude. Don't ever take a job for the money. Take it to learn and progress to where you want to go in life. A job pays in more than financial ways. It may teach you that you do not want to do something. Mom took a job as an assistant chef for six months because we were thinking of opening a restaurant. What she learned is that we did not want to own a restaurant at that point in our lives. Was this a waste? No way! She learned that a restaurant may have greatly hindered other goals in our lives at that time. Plus she learned some great sauces and dishes that she can cook for us. Don't waste even a year of your life working just for "good money."

If you take some time to learn these things now, the benefits will start immediately and pay over your whole life.

Love, Dad

A Hammer to the Head

Hey Kid,

When I was nine years old, I had a bad accident while riding my bicycle down a steep hill. I was taken home by a young man and Mom called the doctor. (That was when doctors still made house calls.) After checking me over, the doctor stood by my bed and discussed with my parents how best to treat me. I do not recall everything they considered, but the one word I have never forgotten was "clamps." The doctor said he might have to put clamps in my head because one of the cuts was so bad.

My image of a clamp was a big staple that the doctor would hammer into my head to hold it together. I was terrified. The longer they talked, the more scared I got. They finally decided to just bandage my head, but that was the worst fifteen minutes of my young life. Nobody explained to me what a clamp was. If they had just included me in the discussion and explained it as they went, it would have been just another incident in my little life. Instead, it has been one of those traumatic things I have never forgotten from my childhood.

Another incident comes to mind along this same line. When I was training as an Emergency Medical Technician in a hospital emergency room, a boy of about seven was brought in with a high fever. This boy was the worst behaved child I had handled in my training. He fought us every step of the way through a simple examination. It took four of us to take his temperature because he fought so hard. He screamed and hit us. When the doctor ordered a shot, he went berserk. Again, four of us held him while a nurse gave him a shot in his fanny. When she was done and we let him go, he jumped up, frantically trying to see his behind. "Is all my blood draining out?", he cried. The boy thought he was going to deflate like a balloon when that needle pierced his skin. I about cried for him. None of us recognized his fear. We all attributed the behavior to his being a bratty kid, but he thought he was going to die.

The lessons of these two stories are important when you deal with children. Adults need to include them in discussions of the decisions that affect their lives. We need to recognize their ignorance of what we take for granted because of our experience. We need to make sure they understand exactly what is going to happen in situations in which they are involved.

Without our input, children draw their own "logical" conclusions based on how they interpret the information available to them. They are not passive entities who totally trust adults without question. They need information just as we do.

Love, Dad

When a Friendship Fails

Hey Kid,

Got your letter about your friends. Tough subject because it is so broad. Let me try to offer some core ideas for you to consider about friends. You will have to apply them to each of your relationships. That I cannot do for you.

First of all, friends can be wonderful or tremendously disappointing whether they are young or old. This is a matter not of age, but of maturity. No, they will not necessarily get better as you get older.

True friends are rare in this life, but this is not an indictment of everyone. As Martin Buber wrote, we are lucky to have one or two "I/Thou" relationships in our life. I think the reason is that each of us sees everything from a unique self-view. You see your relationship with Mom and me totally from your direction, and we see the same relationship totally from ours. It is harder to see such differences in a friendship between two people the same age and with many of the same interests, thus the disappointments.

I think all people enter into friendships for their own benefit. This is not a cynical opinion, just reality. As the relationship grows, each person becomes more concerned with the other's needs, and a true give/take relationship begins to form. This takes a lot of effort and not everyone is willing or able to do this. When one person gives more than the other, the imbalance can cause pain or frustration to both, not just the giver. The loss of benefit from the friendship can end the need for the relationship.

After many great disappointments with my friends, I have now taken this approach: I try to see the really neat things in each person while recognizing their limitations. Then I am not disappointed later. My good friend Ken is a tremendously hard worker. He and I have done many difficult jobs together, and we each enjoyed working with another craftsman. Since I quit going to bars with him at night, he no longer calls me to help him on his projects or stops by our house. I really miss him and told him so. He said I just wasn't any fun now. Should I not like him? No. I am disappointed, but still respect him as a craftsman, and I will always value the time we spent together. Few friends stay with you through all the changes and trials in your life. Do not hold it against them. If someone does, cherish that person and make sure you let them grow and change also.

When a friendship fails or slowly fades, ask yourself what part you played in that. What did you contribute? Were you truly a friend or did you just need a friend? What really caused the end of the relationship? Maybe it was the "great while it lasted" type and nothing could keep it together. The last thing you want to do is to blame the other side and lose the great memories and benefits you gained from them.

I would not teach you how to control friends and cannot guarantee that the good ones will always be there. I can only show you how to maximize the friendships and hope one or two may last a lifetime.

Love, Dad

Who Needs the Discipline

Hey Kid,

I just can't believe these parents who tell their children not to do something ten times in a row. It happens all the time in our store. I think it is the parents who may need the discipline. I don't know if they are just too lazy to properly discipline their children or if they're actually afraid they might lose the child's love if they do.

I doubt if you remember because I started very early with you, but I would tell you not to touch things in stores. If you did it again, we would immediately leave the store and let Mom shop by herself. Also, if you threw a tantrum, I would send you to your room or leave the restaurant or shop where we were. Then I would tell you to cry as long as you wanted, but you were not going to interfere with other people's lives when you did. Needless to say, these behaviors did not last long because you gained nothing by those actions. You also learned to respect other people's property and time.

I think the key to this immediate response discipline was that you always received a reason for the rules we had. I hate the statement, "You do it because I said so." Unexplained rules teach nothing but fear of punishment if they are broken.

Parents who do not offer the real reasons for rules show no concern for their child's emotional and social development.

Some parents are afraid of losing their children's love if they discipline too much. They don't understand the tremendous bond they have with their child. Regardless of the statements or actions of a child ("I'll hate you if you don't let me do that!"), the child knows he is acting badly and that the parent is correct. When I was little, I always knew when I was wrong and that I deserved the discipline I received. I was fortunate to have very fair parents who always explained their reasons to me. They knew, as I did with you, that disciplining will not cost love, but actually increase it.

Some parents seem to be threatened by other adult figures in the child's life, such as a grandparent or teacher. They feel they must be nicer than the other person to keep the child's love. Typical is the grandparent who does not discipline at all and then the parents feel like the "bad guy" when they do. Never let anyone else's actions affect how you relate to your child. Your child can learn much from others, but you are ultimately the most powerful influence on your child.

Never try to buy your child's love. If he or she wants an expensive pair of shoes that you cannot afford, simply explain why you cannot do that. Do not give in out of fear that your child will resent you, and don't promise to buy something else if she or he will stop whining about the shoes. If you cannot afford something, a lesson is learned by stating that and moving on. Of course, your lifestyle should match what you are imposing. Children are very sensitive to unfairness. Discipline is such a big issue that I will have to write more later.

Love, Dad

Stopping a Tragedy

Hey Kid,

In a past letter I told you about a few classes everyone should take. Here's a follow up which you knew was coming because of my past emergency and rescue work. Still, I have to say it.

Everyone, and I mean everyone, should take First Aid and CPR courses. There is no excuse for not doing this. It applies to every person regardless of social status, education, race or whatever. All our bodies work the same, can be hurt the same, and can be cared for the same.

I hope you never need emergency training, but the odds are that you will many times in your life. I pray you will not let someone go without care or die because you did not take the time to learn how to help. Anyone with any kind of a conscience would feel horrible if their lack of a simple class cost another person their life or permanent injury.

My friend, Danny, was washing his four-year-old son in a sink in their apartment. The son reached over and touched the lighted medicine cabinet above the sink. The cabinet had an electrical short in it and instantly the boy collapsed into his father's arms. Danny checked his breathing and pulse. He was not breathing. Danny gave his son three breaths of mouth-to-mouth and the boy started to breathe again on his own. Danny said that if he had not taken CPR, he would have driven his son to the hospital. By that time it would have been too late. One three-hour course for Danny spared him a true tragedy. Incidentally, Danny still took his son to the hospital just to make sure he was okay.

Another friend, Greg, was the first to reach a young girl who had gone through a plate glass window and severed the artery in her thigh. Greg literally reached in and pinched the artery shut, holding it until she arrived in the hospital emergency room. They said the girl would have bled to death if not for his one simple act. Training is what saved these lives.

Another class I believe should be mandatory is a water lifesaving course. Three times in my life I have had to rescue drowning people when there were no lifeguards immediately available. One time the victim panicked and grabbed me tightly. I was afraid we were both going to drown. But my training had taught me that the last place a drowning person wants to be is under water. So I pulled him under until he let go. Then he was ready to listen to me. I talked him out of his panic and he let me pull him to safety. The point is that my training saved both of us. I was sixteen at the time, he was fifteen. What a waste of young lives that would have been if we both had drowned.

Some day you may need to save a member of your family, a friend or a total stranger. Don't go the rest of your life regretting you did not make time to take a few classes.

Love, Dad

Negative Secrets

Hey Kid,

Sure was great to see you last week. The best part for me was the conversation we had out on the campus bench. I was relieved to finally tell you about some of the very negative things in my past. I didn't want you to hear them from anyone else first. I am so thankful that you base your love and respect for me on who I am now and how I have tried to become a man of integrity. We both know that I cannot change my past, but that doesn't mean I should give up on becoming a better man now and in the future.

Having secrets in your life can be destructive to you and those around you. Sure, there are fun secrets like surprise parties or waiting to tell your husband or parents that you are pregnant, but negative secrets force you to tell lies and alter your behavior constantly. They create stresses and give away the power to control your own life.

Imagine a politician who accepts a donation based on his voting a certain way. Now he has to create justifications to his constituents about why he voted that way. He has to live with the constant lies. The pressure must be terrible. The same is true for the unfaithful spouse who then must constantly come up with excuses to be away at certain times. These people have to continually be on guard in their conversations and actions. Is it worth it? From my personal experience, I don't think so.

Negative secrets force you to lie and then lie again to cover the first lie. Lies snowball quickly, and soon it is easier to avoid the people you have to keep deceiving. Many a relationship has been broken or damaged this way. It would have been so much better to not have the secret or admit to it and save those you love the anguish.

When you share a secret or do it in collaboration with someone else, you give that person power over you. You become a hostage to their goodwill. You lose the ability to totally control your own destiny because you are dependent on their willingness to keep your secret. For example, a young man wants to spend the night with his girlfriend. He asks a friend to say he is staying at the friend's house all night. The young man had better not have an argument with his friend in the future or his parents may find out that he was not where he said. He has given his friend a power over him that may force him to alter his true behavior in the future. The friend may force him to lie in the future when the friend needs a favor.

To control your own life, to have people totally trust you, to avoid unnecessary stress in your life, do not have negative secrets. They are never worth it. If you choose to have them, remember, you are choosing a life of deceit. This is why I wanted to clear the air with you on my past. It was worth the risk of losing your love and respect. At least now you can trust your dad even if you don't like some of his past actions.

Love, Dad

Go Ahead and Quit

Hey Kid,

I hate the attitude this society has toward young people. The government, the schools, even churches constantly seem to tell the young they are not capable until they are eighteen. It is no wonder that we have so many problems with youth; they are just living up to what we expect.

By law I can't hire a person under eighteen because he might hurt himself using an electric drill or other power tool. I understand why child labor laws were written, but not why they were written the way they were. Why take the opportunity to learn skills and earn money away from someone just because there are some bad employers around? It would make more sense to let the kids work and learn, but bust the heck out of business owners who try to abuse them. Our laws seem to tell young people that they are incompetent, that they can't do anything without hurting themselves.

I was working construction at thirteen. The foreman and other men taught me the right and safe way to do things. If I did not live up to their standards, I would be fired. I worked hard to live up to what those men expected of me. They protected me as they protected each other. I also did not want to do childish things that may have jeopordized my job. Drugs and alcohol were out of the question because I was expected to perform.

When I taught high school kids Emergency Medical Technician level emergency care, I was really tough on them because lives could be at stake someday. I also believed they were capable of giving care as well as many older people. Some of the new kids complained. They didn't have to work that hard in school and did not see why they should for my program. I said the schools did not work them up to their potential, and that was a shame. They could quit my program anytime they wanted since it was voluntary. I refused to lower my expectations below what I thought they were capable of doing.

All of my complainers stayed with me and worked hard. They developed into a competent team and often administered real emergency care effectively. They just needed someone to believe in them and then drive them to levels of performance they had not experienced before. The trust I placed in their capabilities erased any doubt as to whether I believed in them or not.

If this society would first believe in young people and then offer training and faith, many would live up to it. Some would not, but the same is true for adults.

Believe in your children and other young people. Then give them the skills to live up to your faith in them.

Love, Dad

Take Control from the Big Guys

Hey Kid,

The other day it was hotter than all get out and one of my roofers and I took an hour lunch instead of our usual half hour. He is a senior in college and said he took the job with me to pay off his credit card bill. I must have looked somewhat amazed because he said, "Can you believe that credit card company gave a college student with no job a $1500 credit limit?" He said they should not have given him more than a $500 limit and, as soon as he paid it off, he was going to ask them to cut his limit to that.

He didn't say how much he owed, but I had a feeling he had hit the $1500 limit. He was blaming the card company for his excessive debt. This attitude never ceases to amaze me.

I told him that it was his own fault, not the credit card company's. Of course, he knew that and agreed, but was still going to lower his limit so it could not happen again. I said, if he did that, he would not grow as a person. He asked what I meant; to him, he would keep himself from getting into debt again.

It is a matter of personal responsibility. He was letting someone else control his credit limit instead of himself. I said he should keep the $1500 limit but never use over $500 of it.

Then he would be the one in control and would grow as a person by imposing the discipline upon himself. A year from now, if he succeeded, he would feel better about himself and know that he had the ability to control his spending without outside limitations. This would help him all his life. Letting the credit card company do it would only help this year, and he still would not know if he could control his own debt.

The real issue, I told him, was controlling his own life. If he gives it up on this issue, how many other people or agencies will he allow to control his actions?

I know this issue of "controlling your own life" keeps coming up like a broken record in my letters and conversations with you, but nothing counts without it. It just isn't money issues, either. If you think others control your emotions, then their actions determine when you will be angry, sad, and happy. You will be at the mercy of their actions for how you feel that day. If you think you can't learn a subject because of a bad teacher, you will stay uneducated. It's endless. It is a wasted life that depends on others.

Pay the price in effort and discipline to learn control rather than give it away. Each time you take responsibility for yourself makes it easier to do the next time. Soon you will cherish your self-control and wonder why you ever blamed anyone for what happens in your life. People can inconvenience you, but they can never take control of you without your permission.

Love, Dad

Call Me Lucky

Hey Kid,

Had another person call me lucky because I have my own business, have traveled to different parts of the world, and live in such a wonderful place as Blowing Rock. That statement amazes me because Mom and I really don't have that much wealth. Our net worth in dollars is probably lower than his.

Value choices determine where I spend my money. I believe experiences, people, and learning are more important than material things. In the early '70s I went on a cruise to the Bahamas. The total trip cost $700 for two of us. A friend of mine was saying how lucky I was to be able to do that. He said this while we were watching football on his brand new $700 color TV with stereo record player and radio. I pointed out that I had a black and white TV that I bought used for $35 four years ago. It was not luck. It was simply that he chose to watch TV in color rather than go to the Bahamas.

The most dramatic example, however, is probably our van. I bought it new in 1983. I had it undercoated, rustproofed and all that stuff. When I finally sold it in 1995, it had 360,000 miles on it. Many people trade in their cars after 100,000 miles. If I had done that I would have purchased three more vans during those 12 years. If each one had averaged $20,000 to purchase that would have been an additional $60,000 plus sales tax of $3000. The interest I would have paid for financing those three additional vans would add at least another $20,000. The difference in insurance rates for my van and the three newer ones would have been another $17000. That is $100,000 in after-tax dollars!

I would have to earn at least $120,000 to have the money to own new vans. Basically I gave myself a $10,000 raise each of those twelve years and did not even have to work for it.

That "unearned income" gave us a tremendous advantage over other people earning the same amount as Mom and I. We could put you into a private school that was great for you. We could live through financial ups and downs that would have legally bankrupted us if we owed for cars and furniture and other things. That money gave us the freedom to make choices that our friends could not even think about. We started our store with less than that amount.

So I do not consider myself lucky at all. I just choose certain ways to live that afford me a much richer life in non-material areas like freedom of work choice, travel, education for you, and the ability to try new things without risking total financial ruin. To me those are very easy choices to make in life and the rewards are wonderful.

By the way, I bought a truck six months ago for $700 and have earned over $12,000 with it. Need I say more?

Love, Dad

Special Olympics

Hey Kid,

A little boy with Down's Syndrome came into our store this week. I always get such a warm feeling when I see one of those "special" people. I remember fondly the twelve years I worked at the Special Olympics as a medic in the First Aid Station. Those times were some of the best in my life.

Special Olympics will put more smiles on your face and tears in your eyes than any other thing you can do. Special people are the most appreciative and loving group I have ever been around. They always have a hug for you along with those wonderful smiles. They are so honest in showing their emotions that you cannot but wonder why we live so tight with our emotions and feelings for others. Special people thank you for tying their shoe and hold on tight when they are hurt. Working with them, you are touched by the depth and purity of their love for life and those around them.

One of the most emotional things I have ever seen is the tumbling event at Special Olympics. Many of those athletes were not even capable of remembering their routines. Their coaches would crawl beside them and cue each maneuver as they went along. But at the end of the routine, the Olympian would stand and bow with a proud smile and often with tears

81

of joy to face a roaring crowd. They had done it. Months of practice, fear, and anticipation all came down to two minutes that changed them forever.

There was a little five-year-old who somehow was put in a fifty-yard dash with three ten-year-olds. When the gun went off, the older runners left him in their dust, but he ran his heart out. He stopped right in front of the finish line and stared at it, never looking at anyone else. Then he jumped over it, raised his hands in the air "Rocky" style, and yelled, "All right!" He ran his race and won by finishing it. I am not sure he even heard the crowd going nuts. It was one of those premier moments of life, and I felt so privileged to see it.

The only people more special than "special kids" may be those teachers and aides and counselors who work with them every day. The patience and love these workers have for their "kids" is awesome. Since I worked on many injured and ill Olympians I had the opportunity to watch these workers close up and, often, in very intense situations. They are my heroes. My little volunteer work could not even scratch the surface of the depth of care and love given by these men and women.

If you ever get discouraged by life, go volunteer for the Special Olympics. You will not stay down. You will discover what real love is. You will be thankful for such wonderful people.

Love, Dad

I Like Getting Old

Hey Kid,

Thanks for the birthday card. Hard to believe I'm fifty-four. I know some people dread turning fifty. It is as if life is over for them. I have enjoyed each decade of my life, but none has been feared or dreaded.

The great thing about being in my fifties is the experience level. It seems like this is the decade of my life where experience is paying many dividends.

Experience brings many benefits. First, it gives you confidence. You learn that almost anything is possible. It is no longer a matter of "if I can do something," but "how I can do it." After many attempts at projects, I have found out that, if it is important enough, there is always a way to do it.

Secondly, experience saves you time. I have learned the right and wrong way to approach things. I have also discovered that many of the idealistic ways don't accomplish things. Most things just take hard work. You learn there are no easy ways and so you don't waste time trying them.

Third, experience changes your perspective and values. It taught me that it is more effective to deal with one person at a time if you want to help people. These great big programs don't seem to really touch people. They may sound good, but often they only benefit those administering the programs.

One of the great conflicts between youth and adults is this issue. Young people tend to look at older people as dream killers. As soon as a young person talks of a great dream they have, the older person starts telling them why it won't work or all the problems they will face. The adult's experience is talking. I think it is very hard to try to give advice to youth and make it sound like you still believe in their dreams. A young person should listen very carefully to advice from experienced (and that is the key word) adults. Adults should try very hard to teach how to reach dreams realistically.

Finally, do not forget to look hard at your own experience — it is already very valuable. Some would laugh at the "experience level" of a nineteen-year-old, but I do not. You have probably lived one-fourth of your life already. You have seen young people die. You have had good friends and bad. You have learned that people are not always what they seem: teachers who don't really care about their students, parents who only tolerate their children, and wise young people who see issues better than the adults around them.

Build on this experience. Use it wisely and don't be deceived by the social systems that say you are not competent yet. You may not have many types of life experience yet, but the ones you have had are too valuable not to learn from; they'll pay dividends also.

Love, Dad

Selfish Parents

Hey Kid,

Your roommate told me that you took her to meet Mr. J. She was as impressed with him as I am. I am glad you shared him with her because he is one of those special people in this world. I just want you to know how glad I am that you have him in your life. I think some fathers resent other men in their daughters' lives. I may have at a younger age when I wasn't as secure. Now I realize that I cannot offer you all the wonderful things that are out there. That is why I appreciate people like Mr. J. so much.

I love art, but cannot teach you art. I love theater, but cannot bring out your talents. Mr. J can do these things for you and I am thrilled, not threatened, by that. I love to write and taught you a little about plot and character, but soon realized how limited my skills were for your needs. Mrs. McGinnis's teaching skills made me look like a kindergarten writer. And that was okay because your development was more important than my ego.

I recently visited a friend who has a 16-month-old daughter. She and I hit it off and played on the floor with blocks and all those gadgets they have now for infants. My friend said to his wife, "She likes him more than me!" He just wasn't thinking. He was more worried about his ego than his daughter experiencing new people and having fun. I think it is sometimes hard for parents, especially fathers, to accept that they alone cannot give all that their child needs. It is a very selfish and limiting attitude. Children love their parents more than anyone, but they can still learn from others and enjoy their company.

I know a doctor who will not let his daughter do anything that might physically hurt her. She could not even play soccer as a child. Now she is in college and doing all kinds of things like skiing and riding motorcycles. She never tells her parents because she doesn't want a lecture or to be threatened to be taken out of school. What a shame. These parents are missing some of the best parts of their daughter's life because they are too protective of her. She would love to share these parts of her life, but is afraid to do so.

When you are a parent, try desperately to do what is best for your children. Make sure you are protecting them, not yourself.

I am so thankful for the people like Mr. J and Mrs. McGinnis in your life. You are so lucky to have them. Of course, they are also lucky to have you — someone who appreciates what they have to offer.

Love, Dad

The Money Trap

Hey Kid,

When I was nine years old, I had a bicycle that was becoming pretty shoddy looking. So, I took some of the money that I earned selling Christmas cards and tied into that old bike. I sanded it down, painted it complete with stripes, and added new pedals with reflectors, handle grips with streamers, and a new back reflector. It was the biggest project of my young life. I was so proud of myself. I rode it to the local park the next day to go swimming. When I got out of the pool, it was gone! I cried, Mom and Dad called the police, and the bike was recovered in a couple of days, to my great joy. I immediately went out and bought a lock and chain. I had learned my first lesson about the costs of having nice things. I call it the money trap. The more you have, the more you spend to keep it. When you acquire material things, you must look at the total cost of the item, not just its initial cost.

If you buy a very expensive car, the insurance is part of the cost because you must protect it from damage and theft. If you buy a very expensive home and furnish it beautifully, you insure it to protect against potential fire or storm damage. You would also probably install a security system. You must maintain your property with landscaping and roofs. The amount of effort it takes to maintain material wealth is amazing. And we are not even taking into account the mental stress or concerns that come with that territory. If you put your money into stocks or businesses, you have to pay accountants, brokers, and insurance people to make sure that losses do not financially destroy your family.

We pay a dear price in this country to maintain material things. If we spent the same effort on family, friends and helping others, we would be much "wealthier" and happier people.

I am not saying that material things are bad. I just want you to be aware of their true costs. You will spend a lot of money and time protecting them. You will have more stress in your life as you accumulate material things. You will always have people who want what you have, whether it is a thief, a relative or the government. You must ask before you make material decisions, "Is this worth the total cost? What is the true cost to my family and myself? How much of my life am I willing to give just to own this thing?"

Your friends and family need you and your time. Make sure you don't spend too much of these valuable commodities on things instead of people. In the end, relationships are all that really matter.

Love, Dad

Hurting Others

Hey Kid,

I was talking to one of our employees who turns twenty-one this week. All of her friends want to take her out and get her drunk. Sue just wants to have a glass of wine with dinner and have fun with her friends. She expressed how hard it was to avoid the peer pressure to drink while in college. That led into a discussion of where the line is between right and wrong. Her parents had been so protective of her with all their rules that she had hardly done anything fun, but she wasn't sure how far to go.

I offered my rule for life on deciding each situation. It can be applied to nearly all of life's twists and turns. I always try to act in a way that does not hurt anyone, including myself. This works for me and, when I fail to abide by that standard, I know I am wrong, not someone else.

If Sue got drunk against her wishes, she would not feel good about herself and would never be able to look back at her twenty-first birthday with fondness. That sounds very minor, but it is not. She would hurt herself by losing her good memories and knowing she did not control her own life that night.

It is easy to know that sticking a gun in someone's face and demanding money is wrong. But what about goofing off at work or not doing the quality of work that is expected of you? This is also stealing from someone. You are taking money from your boss or the customer that you did not earn. Some people do not consider that stealing, but what else is it?

After you were born, I had to reevaluate many things that I did. A very minor one was how I drove my motorcycle. I found myself being much more careful because I had to take care of you and Mom. Getting in an accident would affect more lives than only mine. Now if I got stupid on that bike and broke a leg, I would not be able to provide as well for you.

This rule will also help in your relationships. Do your actions contribute to making the relationship better? If you lie or argue or do not share, are you hurting your friend, spouse, child? I think each of us knows when we hurt the other person in a relationship, no matter how we rationalize our actions.

The applications of this guideline are endless. You can use this every day of your life: how you do your work, who you choose as friends, how you speak and act to those around you, how hard you work, what kind of parent and spouse you are every day.

The part of this rule that is easily missed is not to hurt yourself. It is often harder to see the real hurt you do to yourself. Let's talk about that one later.

Love, Dad

Hurting Yourself

Hey Kid,

Wanted to get back to you on the second part of my rule for deciding if something is right or wrong. I said that you should not do anything that hurts others or yourself. The hurting yourself part can be tricky sometimes.

I had a sharp young man working for me. He always came to work on time, worked hard, and was inquisitive about how to do things right. One Saturday he did not show up at all. It just didn't fit and I was worried that something may have happened to him. I finally got him on the phone Sunday and he told me this story about having to go out of state to bail a friend out of jail. It didn't quite make sense that he had not called to let me know, but I chalked it up to his youth. I explained how worried I was about him and also how his not being there affected the job and my ability to provide for my family. He said he was sorry and that it would not happen again.

About a month later he did not show up again. This time I made some calls and found out that one of his friends came to town and they had gone out drinking. Now I think he may have a drinking problem, but I do not know for sure. He has never called me since then and obviously has not come back to work. I think he was too ashamed to face me.

The sad thing is that he not only lost his job, but he lost my respect. He will never be able to look back and laugh about all the good times we had together. He still lives near me and must dread the possibility of running into me somewhere. He hurt himself more than he did me.

These situations are endless in life. Try to think through the complete ramifications of your actions for others and for yourself. I learned this the hard way and would like to help you avoid that.

You won't always get it right. When you do hurt someone, there is really only one way to correct these hurts. That is make amends. Have the courage to say you were wrong and ask to be forgiven. This not only helps whomever you have hurt, but it eases the hurt you caused yourself. The key here is to be truly repentant. Asking forgiveness without changing your future actions is a joke. Repentance demands change.

I didn't think I could ever forgive myself for some things I had done, but I worked to produce an actual change of behavior in my life. Sometimes it took me years to believe I had changed. At first I did not trust that the change was real.

Many times you cannot correct the damage you have done. The only thing you can offer is living differently so that type of thing does not happen again.

Love, Dad

"Stupid Tickets"

Hey Kid,

You reached the twenties all in one piece — pretty good! Hope you had a great time on your birthday. Sure was fun to talk to you on the phone.

I am proud of you for so many things. One came up the other day even without you here. I was at my insurance agent's office talking about my business and then our personal auto insurance came up in the conversation. The agent said that our rate will go down substantially because you have driven four years without one traffic ticket. She thought that was great for a young person.

I told her that you and I had a conversation about tickets when you started driving. I said that getting traffic tickets was about the stupidest thing a person could do. Tickets are one of the most unnecessary aggravations in life. It is so easy to avoid them. Drive the speed limit, stop at the right places, and think safety and consideration for the other people on the road. These are also the reasons none of us has had an accident.

I related the story to her of driving to the "big city" 30 miles away when I was sixteen. I always drove like crazy on that two-lane road and worried about getting caught. On one trip my friend, Bill, said speeding probably did not save us very much time. So we timed it. I drove like crazy going there and then stayed on the speed limit on the way back. The difference was four minutes! What a great lesson for me.

Later I figured if I have to travel 55 miles and I go 55 miles per hour, it obviously will take me one hour. If I go 65, it would only save me nine minutes. At 80 miles per hour, I would save 19 minutes. What a joke. I not only risk a ticket and all the stress of watching out for the police, but I put myself and others at risk for the sake of a few minutes. I have also learned how much longer my cars last when they are driven safely. The suspensions do not wear out as fast, tires and brakes go more miles, and cars do not use as much gasoline.

The intangible benefits are equally as good. I know that I can be a far better defensive driver when I first obey the laws. I arrive where I am going relaxed and feel good that I am in control of the safety of my life and my passengers. Sound hokey? It isn't. It's a nice, comfortable way to drive and live.

So I am proud of you as a driver. Your record shows you keep your senses about the serious business of driving. It also shows that you are concerned about others and do not endanger them with your driving. Keep it up. There is enough in life to be worried about without getting "stupid tickets," which is what we should call them. Maybe then people would be too ashamed to get them.

Love, Dad

Afraid for You

Hey Kid,

Sounded like your trip to Boston went great. Now that you're back, let me say how hard it is for me, as a parent, when you do trips like these. I am not complaining, honestly. I did the same types of things when I was eighteen and lived through them all.

It sure is different being on this side of a child/parent relationship. While I have complete trust in your travel and driving skills, I naturally worry about all those "unknowns" that are out there. They could also happen to me or Mom, but when it's my child, it doesn't seem the same.

I think one of the hardest things for a parent is to let your child take risks, whether it is going swimming with the gang or driving 800 miles by herself. The problem is not to protect your child from life itself. Most of the really neat things in life involve risk, whether it is loving someone, traveling to Papua New Guinea or rapelling cliffs. If you never take a risk, you live a very sheltered life. In a sheltered life you can still get hurt, emotionally or physically, but sheltered people don't have the experience to cope with the pain.

I think we have to let our children take risks within their capability and let them get hurt so they will grow to handle life.

Remember when I told you to make physical contact while playing soccer instead of shying away at the last moment? You were only nine, the only girl on the field, and had never been very physical. I asked you to make contact only three times during the game. You jumped into the action at least that many times and came out smiling at what you had accomplished. Yes, you got your shins kicked a couple of times and broke your glasses, but you were a different person having taken the risk. You discovered you could be physical and felt a pride of accomplishment knowing you had truly helped your team. From then on soccer was much more fun for you.

As a parent, you find out how selfish you can be when it comes to your child's life. All you want to do is protect your child from everything that can go wrong. I think the real reason is to spare us, the parents, from the fear of watching someone we love so much get hurt. We stunt our child's growth to protect ourselves from that pain. I often had to seriously question my motives to make sure I was protecting you and not me.

Let your children get their shins kicked once in a while. They will be far better people in the end. It is too easy to "protect" your children, creating unequipped adults who can not make good decisions because they never suffered the consequences of risk-taking.

Keep on trying out life in all its magnificence. I will be thrilled for what you accomplish and learn. I also will always be afraid for you and would love to protect you from being hurt. Your job is to forgive my selfish fears for you.

Love, Dad

Emotions Are Your Choice

Hey Kid,

Had one of those poignant moments that pop up in life. I was at a benefit steak dinner. The event was at the local VFW and attended by many people who were not members. The tables sat ten each and it was fun meeting new people. The commander of the VFW came up and was complaining to a couple of us local members that someone had parked in the handicap space again. He was quite agitated about this and was threatening to get the car towed away.

A gentleman across the table said that he was the offending party parked in that spot and that he would move the car. The commander was so angry that he just stared at the man. The man started to get up and grabbed his crutches, which none of us had seen. The whole table broke up laughing while the commander looked on sheepishly. The man with the crutches joined the laughter and the commander was then able to laugh at himself.

The real issue here was the commander's choice of emotions. The car did not cause the emotion. He changed immediately when he saw the owner was handicapped. All of us choose our emotions based on our beliefs or needs.

It would be nice if other people determined our reactions; it's always easier to blame them than to be responsible for our own actions. But, whatever someone does, it's still our choice how we feel about it. Let's say a guy told ten random people that they were stupid. Chances are high that he would get ten different reactions. Some would be upset, some amused, some merely baffled. But if emotions were truly dictated by circumstance, wouldn't they all react identically? No such luck.

You can't give up responsibility for your emotions without giving up freedom. I'd rather have the chance to mess up on my own than let other people mess up for me. I do not want to permit them the power to control my emotions because then they control my life.

Emotions are tricky and have to be dealt with carefully. All have a place, but those that can be negative should be used in small doses; too much intensity in any direction can cause trouble. As a general rule, sorrow is better than anger; anger is preferred to rage. Likewise, disappointment is better than depression.

Sometimes it's hard to decide what response is the best one, but don't forget that other people can offer valuable insight to your decisions without controlling them. I am here and there are always professional third parties. The initial awkwardness of talking to a counselor will still be far better than the possible consequences of a bad emotional choice.

Love, Dad

Glue for Marriage

Hey Kid,

I just love working in the store with your mother. It's not just because she's good-looking, either. We really have fun together.

I think it is more than our personalities or experience in dealing with the public. We share so many values and attitudes that there are no conflicts in how we approach our business and customers. The harmony of values results in the security and trust we have in each other. In that atmosphere we are so comfortable and happy that our customers feel it and respond positively to us.

Both of us know that we do not cheat people, that we give true value for the dollar, and that most of our customers are interesting people. Think of the conflicts that would occur if only one of us felt that way.

I think the successes in our marriage have come from our compatibility of values in many key areas. For a marriage to work, there must be agreement on the basic premises of life. You can never agree if you start from different points of view unless one of you changes your attitude.

A good example of this problem is also probably the biggest conflict in many marriages — how to handle money. If one partner believes you never go into debt and pay all your bills before you have fun and the other one does not, look out. Who makes the decisions then on how to spend the money? This issue will affect everything from what kind of food you eat and what you drive to where you live and how you dress. There will be hardly one issue that money does not affect. Without agreement on this issue, there will be constant conflict and tension.

Money is closely tied to integrity. Integrity is probably the core issue in most areas of marriage. One of the partners may believe it is okay to "get away" with cheating at sports or taxes or traffic laws. This will constantly irritate the other partner who believes that is wrong. It will affect how they raise their children, the friends they choose, and whether they can work together in business. Each must have the same level of personal integrity to make mutual decisions on almost everything they do.

Your mother and I have a tremendous advantage in our marriage by agreeing on issues of money, children, how to treat others, working for material things versus life experience. We have some long, hard discussions, but there is never any long-term problem in our approach to many of these key areas. The fact that both of us want a life of integrity makes resolution possible on many issues. The resulting fun and comfort level with each other is a wonderful way to live.

Love, Dad

Go With Your Nature

Hey Kid,

Been thinking about your "finding something to do" letter. I know I've already said "do whatever you do with integrity and care for those in your life." I still think these are great guidelines for being fulfilled in whatever you do, but let me add two more thoughts to those.

First, I think it is important to choose what is right for yourself, not just what is available. If a sports magazine offered me a writing job, that would be nice. But you and I both know that it would not be a great job for me no matter what the salary and perks. I would do better to keep searching for a writing position about travel or young people or emergency care. I love these subjects. They would be right for me. You must not only search for what you are capable of doing, but for what is rewarding to you.

Go with your true nature, not just your education. Education can mean formal, societal, or on-the-job training of what you "should" be. I would love to write fiction and am presently trying to do that. But I have to ask myself, "Am I truly a fiction writer?" I am still not sure. My best education from lifelong experience is as a contractor, businesswise and skillwise. Yet the one word I would use to describe myself is

103

"teacher." I love to teach. I work hard at it, enjoy it, and grow with it. So maybe I should write teaching type novels or non-fiction. This is my true nature, though not my education.

My second thought is to remember "the good is ever the enemy of the best." Too many people, including me, have done really good things vocationally or otherwise. The sad thing is that we did not do the best we were capable of doing. Each did well enough not to get fired, get a paycheck, or contribute to an organization. It was acceptable to ourselves and those around us, but we could have been so much more.

I am not talking about being compulsive, having to win every battle and beat everybody in life. Perfection is not the goal — perfection is an illusion. There is a level of excellence in all of us that requires just a little more effort than being good. It does not take two or ten times the effort to go from good to best. It just takes that little extra step that is seldom demanded in life.

Always do the best you can, not just better than the other guy, and don't wait until you are perfect, because you'll die still waiting.

Love, Dad

You're Better Than That

Hey Kid,

"You dummy!" No, not you. That was a statement I heard a father say to his four-year-old son. I am sure that child will believe that he is a dummy if his own father tells him that enough.

How we talk to our children is so important. Of course, we have to discipline and correct them. That is part of our job as parents. But another important part of that job is to teach them self-worth. How do we do both — tell them they are wrong and still help them feel good about themselves?

First, check out how you view your children. Are they capable people with little experience or some kind of being lower than an adult? Our view of children totally affects how we treat and teach them. I believe kids are capable people without much experience in life. They learn correctly and quickly, and how they feel about themselves affects their attitude toward learning.

The statement I use with people who deliberately do a poor job is "You are better than that." This can be said to anyone including children as young as two years old. There are two messages in that short statement. First, I am telling them that their work is not acceptable. The second message is that I believe in them. I am not saying they can't do the work well; I know they can do it correctly. It is important that people, especially children, know you believe in them. Then they can believe in themselves.

Another statement to make to your children when they are acting inconsiderate, like throwing a tantrum or crying because they did not get their way, is "We don't act like that!" I used this with you when you were about two. Again, the statement did not say you were different than us. It affirmed that we could act like that also, but chose not to do so. This sets a standard of behavior and illustrates what is unacceptable.

Your children will believe you, whether they like the message or not, if you live according to the same standards that you place on them. That is why your statements are so important. They have to have faith in their abilities even after they have made a mistake or done less than acceptable work. They must know you still believe in them. Do not assume the child knows this — state it clearly!

It is easy to say you believe in people when they do a good job. It is far more important to let them know you believe in them when they have done less than their best.

Love, Dad

Facing the Gun

Hey Kid,

Faced that big and very real gun again. Had a mole flare up and immediately thought of my Aunt Ginny who died from melanoma. Took over a month to get an appointment with the doctor and then get results back. It was benign. What a relief!

The whole process made me think of Vietnam again. Remember how many times I called war the "great values clarification course"? I came back from that war with such a different view of life. So many things no longer had any importance: money, fame, prestige, fancy cars, "beautiful people." It was just good to be alive. The beauty of a whole and laughing person seemed to be the most wonderful thing in the world. To walk around without other men trying to kill you every minute of every day was an exhilarating freedom. I vowed never to get caught up in money and power plays and materialism again. You know the results. You grew up with that man.

This wait for the biopsy report was again a time of looking at my life and where I am at this point. The strongest emotion was sadness. I was sad about what I might miss with you and Mom.

It seems like this is the best period of my life. You are just starting into true adulthood and all the wonderful potential you bring to it. I am finally writing those books that I thought only other people could write. I no longer fight the demons of rage and guilt I carried home from Vietnam. Mom and I finally have a business together that we enjoy and are very good at doing. Waiting for the test results, I wondered, "Why now? Why not when I was crazy and unproductive?"

I know the answer is simply, "that's life." We used to say in Vietnam, "It don't mean nothing." Was this cynical? I don't think so. We just learned young that you could die very easily in this world and that few things meant much in the whole scope of the universe. We were all going to face the same end someday, some way. That's life.

So what does count? This month, as I again looked at my life, I came to the same conclusions as when I came home in 1969. There are only two things that are important. First, to live each day to the best of your ability and with integrity to yourself and those around you. Second, to love and to be loved intensely.

The first I keep striving for. The second I feel fortunate to have experienced. True, unselfish love between a parent and child is the epitome of life's experiences. The test for melanoma has helped me see my life in perspective again. I have reached the top because of you.

Love, Dad

It's Fun To Be Good

Hey Kid,

Yesterday a friend commented on the energy level that your mother and I have. I think she wonders how we can work so much. Her statement reminded me of what my father used to say: "If you give a lazy man a job that he enjoys, he will work hard." I have hired a few men who might not prove that, but basically I think my father was right. Working hard is often a matter of motivation. If you hate your job, you probably will not work hard at it.

Your mother and I have tried to structure our lives to do what we enjoy. The resulting "work" is simply applying energy to things we like to do. If I won the lottery, I probably would not own a store or have a roofing business, but I know I would still work hard at whatever I chose to do, such as becoming a great bass fisherman or traveler or writer.

There is another dimension at work here, too. Both your mother and I have the attitude that no matter what you do, you should do it to the best of your ability. It is tough to get bored when you are working hard at being good, and it is fun to be good at what you do. You can respect yourself for that and others will respect you. Everyone enjoys being around people who feel good about what they are doing.

After I was drafted into the Army, some of the other soldiers asked me if I was going to make a career of it because I worked so hard. I said, "No way!" I wanted out, but since I had no choice, I was going to make the best of it. They thought I was nuts, but I enjoyed it more than they did, got more promotions, and thus had better jobs to do. The hard work may have saved my life when I got to Vietnam. I was taken out of an infantry platoon and made supply sergeant. I had learned supply while I was stateside, even though it was not my job as an infantry trainer.

If you find yourself always tired and bored at your job, look hard at your life. If you hate your job, change it. If that is not possible, try a different attitude. Decide to be the best that you can be at that job, not for your boss, not for your customers, but for yourself. Remember the parts manual your mother wrote for the boat manufacturer without being asked? She felt so much better doing more than expected. She took a boring job and made it interesting.

If you want energy in your life, do what you enjoy and do it well. It's fun to be good.

Love, Dad

Quality Time is a Myth

Hey Kid,

I was talking with your aunt about a recent children's movie. She wondered if it had too much violence for her son and daughter to see. I watched the tape and it was violent. I felt it wasn't the best for her kids, but they could easily see it at a friend's house without her knowledge.

I always tried to experience things with you that I figured you were going to do anyway. That way I could give my input rather than just hope it did not affect you negatively. You cannot hide the world from your children. They will see it eventually. Plan to be there when it happens.

When a situation came on television like unmarried people hopping in bed together, I told you why I felt that was wrong. I talked about how sad it was when a soldier was killed in battle and how it affected his family. I did not want these things to become commonplace in your mind even if they seemed that way in movies or books.

I remember when you just learned to read and Mom took you into a public bathroom while we were on a trip. You read some graffiti words that you had never seen before and asked what they meant. Mom explained that those were words that we did not use because of their crudeness. There were nicer words to use.

There was also the time that you and Mom saw a cat eating a baby rabbit. Mom explained that it was nature at work, no matter how sad it seemed. You were learning then instead of being traumatized by that scene.

The important key here is spending time, a lot of time, with your children. I don't believe in this "quality time" thing. You cannot plan ahead for all those little, spontaneous events that need discussion when they happen. Can you imagine saying to your six-year-old child, "Today we are going talk about cats eating bunnies"? This is why I believe at least one parent should be home with the children when they are growing up. Life is learned in all the little situations that come up each day. You cannot pre-plan when many issues will need to be discussed. Children need time with you and lots of it.

Obviously, you cannot spend every minute with your children because of school and other events in life. What about those periods of their lives? The answer is the same. Take a lot of time to listen to how their day went, what their friends are doing, what they learned in school. Careful listening will still bring out daily issues that you may want to address.

So, don't try to over-protect your children. It is unrealistic to think you can hide the world from them. Instead, be there when they meet the world.

Love, Dad

Needless Worry

Hey Kid,

Read a neat thing in the "Reader's Digest" a while back. It went something like this: "When I was twenty, I worried what people thought about me. When I was forty, I didn't care what they thought of me. When I was sixty, I realized they weren't thinking about me." What a great synopsis of our changing view of life in relation to other people.

I think all this worry about what others think is taught to the young many ways. Parents often teach their children some very good things, but for the wrong reasons. We were taught to behave correctly so that the preacher or the neighbors or "Aunt Gertrude" would not think badly of us. This is a cop-out way to teach. Parents and other teachers should show the benefits of good behavior, rather than instill the fear of disapproval. The benefits are having more people enjoy being with you, others trusting your personality as true, and pride in being a good, decent person.

These benefits are very difficult to teach in this society. Television constantly says that no one will like you if you don't have a beautiful house or wear great clothes or drive a fancy car. People are accepted more for being part of a group than being "different."

When you are young, you do not have the experience to challenge adult dictates, so it is pretty normal to base your actions on others' opinions. Thus, you worry about what others think about you. When you base your actions on what people think, you give away control of your life.

As you get older and have more life experience, you realize that what you were taught was for the convenience of the older people. They did not want to listen to or take time for a child. As you discover that your opinions and observations are valid, you do not need the approval of others to feel good or confident about yourself. You gain control of your life because you are not basing your decisions and actions on the opinions of others. You learn it is better to make your own choices and possibly be wrong than to let others make your decisions for you. You will grow through your own mistakes. When you make mistakes based on other people's thinking, you will blame them and not have a growth experience for yourself.

Finally you'll realize not many people were thinking about you at all. My friend Joan said years ago that "everyone is a star in their own soap opera." I thought that was a cynical opinion, but now realize she was right and just pragmatic. People have their own lives and really don't go around thinking about whether I have money or am smart or whatever. They are thinking about their lives, their triumphs, their tragedies.

So don't waste your life worrying about what others think. Don't give them that false power over you because they probably don't care as long as your actions do not affect their lives. When you live as who you really are, you will touch them far more than living as they think you should. I want different, refreshing people around me — not ones who are trying to be what they think I want. They are kinda boring.

Love, Dad

Jinx

Hey Kid,

This morning was sad for me. It was the first morning without Jinx following me around as we did our little morning routine together. I know he was kind of a dumb cat, but he was like a puppy in his faithfulness and his predicting my every move each morning. He was always at the door when I got home in the evening and seemed to know when I was going to lay down on the couch. He was right there ready to lay on my legs as I read.

His kidneys were failing. He had lost weight, but we thought it was the new food the vet put him on. Yesterday we went in for the routine shots and found out how sick he was even though he did not act like it. The vet told us she could inject fluids under Jinx's skin and keep him going a little longer. We asked her if there was any hope of recovery at his age and she admitted it was probably a fatal condition. It would have been selfish for us to keep him alive and suffering just so we would not have to decide to put him to sleep right then. The treatment was more for us than Jinx.

It is very hard not to be selfish at a time like that. I would miss him a lot and that was my problem, not something he should suffer for. I would have had a hard time looking you in the eyes if I did not do what was best for him. We always tried to teach you that if you took responsibility for an animal, you had to do it completely. Remember the $200 operation on your pet rat? At that point in our lives, it was a great sacrifice to pay that kind of money, but we felt the lesson to you was even more important.

Pets are a wonderful way to teach children about the preciousness of life. A child can be taught not only that the pet needs food, water and exercise, but that the animal also needs love and concern for its whole life. Any living creature must not suffer unnecessarily and deserves the best care you can give. I believe that a child taught these things will not only learn compassion, but about the life and death cycle. A child does not understand her own or a parent's mortality. A pet is a great way to teach these things and then apply them to human life.

There would be less cruelty and fewer personal crimes against humans if people were taught as children about the value of life. How many criminals, in their childhood, have exhibited cruelty to animals?

Use pets to teach your children that life can be short and to enjoy each day with those that they love. They can learn compassion, caring, and mortality. Jinx was a friend I will miss. His death is part of life's cycle. I am so glad he was part of my life's cycle.

Love, Dad

Points on Your License

Hey Kid,

Hope you got the article I sent you on leasing versus buying a car. You can see it really depends on your lifestyle and how you will use the vehicle, plus the true total costs. It makes me wonder why they don't teach you that kind of stuff in school. People get in so many messes in life that are simply lack of education. It seems to me we could teach young people many practical things to help them later.

A class on simple financial things could change a lot of peoples' lives. At what point do you drop comprehensive insurance on your car and just buy liability? How much life insurance do you need and how will it change as your life progresses? How do you balance a checkbook? The real effects of compound interest and how much money you can save if you understand this.

Let me give you an example of a topic for one class: traffic tickets. Everyone realizes that it will cost you money for the fine and most people know you can get points on your driver's license. But there is much more than that.

First, if you have too many points on your license, your insurance rate goes up. It could get cancelled. Then we are talking dramatic increases for high risk insurance. Many employers cannot hire people with more than four points on their license because the employer's insurance company won't cover those drivers. So tickets can keep you from getting jobs. All the men in my dad's construction company had to drive company vehicles, so no one got hired if they had too many tickets.

Some employers look at the character side of a person with a lot of tickets. Their opinion is that people with several traffic violations are not considerate of those around them. Those drivers are willing to put others at risk and that makes them dangerous employees. They don't really care about anyone else.

The wildest example I ran into was the recruiter for a very specialized military program. I asked him why they cared if someone had a lot of tickets. After all, what they did was extremely dangerous and kinda crazy. He said, "We don't care that they were speeding, but if they have a lot of tickets it means they were careless. They got caught. In our business we cannot have that."

Many people may check what kind of driver you are because it tells much about you. Nobody taught me that in school. I sure would have looked at my driving differently before I learned the hard way. The real reason to drive safely is consideration of others and yourself, but some people need other reasons also.

Love, Dad

Suicide

Hey Kid,

I feel compelled to write to you about a very hard subject—suicide. While I do not think you have ever considered it, it may come up with your friends or loved ones in the future as it did in your past.

To me, suicide is the ultimate selfishness. The horrible part is that the person considering suicide is so wrapped up in his own self that he cannot see beyond his pain. (I am not talking about those near death or in great physical pain from a fatal disease.) Blinding emotional pain is also blind to the pain it causes those who love that person.

I try hard to remember how deep and desperate my pain was when I got crazy about Vietnam. It seemed there was no way to compensate for being alive when so many young men died. Could I have done something better to keep them alive? Nothing could bring them back. I felt their finality should also be mine. It seemed to be the only answer. It was a horrible trap for me. In my twisted thinking, death was the only atonement to them for my being alive.

Was this selfish? Yes. It did not consider the woman who wanted to spend the rest of her life with me. It did not consider the daughter who loved her daddy and would never have another one. It did not even consider the good men I mourned. Not one of them would have wished my death. It would have been a disgrace to them to waste another life because of that war. I would have amplified my pain and spread it to those who meant the most to me. It is still hard for me to forgive myself for my self-centeredness.

If you ever hit a time in your life where you are even considering suicide, I want you to remember those who love you. I want you to remember yourself as an eight-year-old who would have lost her father. I want you to remember the wonderful years you and I have had since then. These are the things that help you see through the haze of pain.

This sounds overly simple, but I believe anyone can endure. For anyone considering suicide, the hard part is believing that you can live with the pain. The hardest is doing the work it takes to survive. The eighteen months of therapy that I went through at the Vet Center were very difficult, but it enabled me to see I wasn't the only one with problems from that war. My pain was no greater than the other guys'. We all helped each other. They helped me save my own life. I found answers to what I thought was unanswerable.

I am so thankful I chose life. It has been wonderful being your father. Your love for me was a big part of my fight to live.

Love, Dad

Accumulating Money

Hey Kid,

Let's talk about something really scary — the marginal utility of money! Actually, it's not scary, it just sounds like it. It is a concept that I learned in an economics course way back in college. It is one of those ideas that stuck with me because I had very little money and was always trying to make more by working an extra job or two.

I do not remember the actual definition, but it has to do with the power of any extra money over and above necessities. That is the money that can change your life style or dreams. I used this when I first started my roofing company. I would work with my men for forty hours a week and that would pay the basic bills for us and the company. Maybe we would have $25 left for extras. Then I would work an additional 10 or so hours by myself and clear an extra $150. The key is that I did not have to work six times as much to get that money. Not even twice as much. I only worked an additional 25 percent to get six times the spending power for the things that would better our lives.

If you get a job out of college that pays $20,000 a year, that means you will probably take home around $1250 per month after taxes. In an oversimplified budget, let's say your rent is

$600 per month including utilities. You will spend $200 on food and $200 more on your car. Add $50 for your phone bill and another $100 for clothes, medicine, etc. and you end up with $100 per month left for savings, fun, or buying things that will better your life. That is the disposable income that will determine a lot of your lifestyle

If you drank one less soft drink a day and made your morning coffee instead of buying it at the bakery, you could easily save $50 per month and increase your extras or savings by half again as much. A three hour per week part-time job could bring in an additional $50 per month. Now you have doubled your disposable income and the ability to change your immediate or future life style.

I watch all kinds of people complaining about not having enough money to do or have something. They often do this while eating out every day instead of packing a lunch. They will go out for a pizza with a friend and spend $20 instead of inviting their friend over and make a pizza that costs six dollars. They just don't realize how fast their extra money could accumulate with a little care in spending habits.

I do not begrudge anyone how they live. I just don't want to hear the complaints when they are not using the power of their extra money efficiently.

When you think times are tough or if you want something better in life, look hard at how to increase your disposable income. Remember the utility of that extra marginal income. Wow, what an academic letter!

Love, Dad

We Did It Again!

Hey Kid,

We did it again! Five wonderful days of nothing to do but hang out together. I love going into your world and seeing all the places and people that have been a part of your life. Hearing about Boston from you these last three months has been fun, but it is so much better to walk the streets together and actually experience it with you.

It is hard to explain to people how we can have so much fun together and "not do anything." Sure, we hit the art museum, the aquarium, and an improv theater, and we ate like crazy at all those great restaurants. But the best part was the walking around and talking and laughing and seeing life in all its many facets.

You and I can enjoy watching the wonderful ways of children and listen to their honest comments. We see the great love stories in couples walking side by side and know they are equal to or greater than the classic ones of literature. We appreciate the friendliness of the shopkeepers in their struggles to provide a living for their families. It's this sharing that makes it so much fun.

I think one of the great strengths of our relationship is that neither of us feel we have to "entertain" the other. I have often wondered how that developed. Sometimes I think it was just luck, but honestly I believe it developed very early. Mom and I were always so excited by all those little things that intrigued you when you were very young. Nothing was "stupid kid's stuff" because your experience level was obviously very limited. We all shared with each other what was exciting to each of us. Now we just keep sharing and know the other respects and enjoys hearing about what we have to say. There is no need to create special conversations to "entertain" the other person. Heck, there is no need for any conversation some of the time!

When you have children, beware of that "quality time" attitude. Some people seem to think that a few hours of planned time with their children makes up for quantity. The parent/child relationship requires time together — a lot of it. Remember how many times you and I went to the mall. We walked slowly and looked at everything and talked. I thought it was important that we did not just run in and buy something and then head on for the next chore. I wanted that time with you because that is where so many great little conversations came up about people, values, and wants. This kind of time together is as significant as going to a museum or a baseball game.

Nothing is more important than time with your children. Nothing will bring greater rewards for the rest of your life. You can never earn enough money to pay for that time in any way. You will never get that time back if you miss it.

Thanks for sharing the Boston part of your life with me. It was so simple, but so special.

Love, Dad

Starting Your Own Business

Hey Kid,

Got a call from Eric. He's in California now. He wanted to talk about starting his own business installing electronic equipment. He has the experience and many of the mental assets to do this right. He just did not know how to begin and is afraid to make the jump. The fear is normal for most folks because it involves leaving the security of a regular paycheck.

I know you have thought about owning your own business someday, so let me share with you what I told him. The first thing is to understand the value of your time. Eric is a conscientious young man and does his work with a craftsman's attitude. This is a valuable asset. I told him to make sure he charges enough for the value he gives to his customers. That he could understand. What he did not think about was that when he goes out to sell a job and work up the estimate, he also needs to pay himself. If I hired a salesman, he would expect to be paid for his time. Also, if I hired a bookkeeper or field superintendent they would have to be paid. Since I always served all these functions I should make sure I pay myself for these services. The mistake most new business people make, especially in contracting, is to charge only for what they actually do on the job. Then at the end of the year they wonder why they are going broke after working their tails off. You have to charge what a big outfit does so you can pay yourself for all the functions a big outfit pays other people to do.

Secondly, and even more important, is to do the job right even if you did not estimate it correctly. The benefits are greater than the money or time loss you may incur. You will have satisfied customers who know they received what they paid for. You will feel good about yourself. It will help with that next sales call because you will have confidence and integrity when you talk about what you can do. You know you will do a good and honest job and it comes through to those around you. It's fun to be good.

When you are trying to do it right, your customers will tolerate mistakes. If you have to go back to make it right, they won't be screaming at you. Most of them know when someone has just made a mistake and did not try to cheat them. No one is perfect. In all the years I have contracted work I have never been sued. This is not from being perfect, but simply from doing it right or going back to fix mistakes.

The nicest result of doing work right is your future relationship with your customers. They are always glad to see you and refer others to you. They send you other good customers because they like you. They don't refer unreasonable people or people who don't pay their bills. I have some great relationships now with people who simply started out as customers.

There are many nuts and bolts about going on your own like licenses, payroll taxes and suppliers. But I think understanding the value of what you have to offer and doing the work with integrity are the two most important things.

Love, Dad

Living Together vs. Marriage

Hey Kid,

I bought Mom some ballpoint pens for the store because she says I steal all of hers. I probably do. She looked at them and asked me if I still had the receipt. She was going to take them back because they had black ink. She likes blue! Can you believe after twenty years of marriage that I just learned this about her?

I think that is what keeps marriage interesting after years and years. There are all those things you never knew about your spouse. Also, changes take place as a natural part of life experience and interaction with each other. Your mother is such a different person from the girl I married, but still the same in so many ways. The interaction of this relationship is still intriguing.

I suppose that is one reason why I am against people living together to see if they will be okay in a marriage. They delude themselves if they think living together for a while is like being married. Marriage is a continuous and ever-changing relationship. It is experiencing things together that are long-term and full of wonderful ups and tragic downs. You do not learn how your partner will handle those things just by living together for a year or two.

So how do you choose someone to commit to for the rest of your life? It is tough because none of us knows another's heart. My advice is to closely observe him in many of the "little" situations in life. How does he treat his family? Is he considerate of them? Does he place a value on being with them? Does he keep himself clean? Have you seen him in volunteer situations? Is it an ego trip or true concern for others? Is he kind to kids and animals? Does he tell off-color jokes or put down certain races or ethnic groups? Does he pinch or punch you hard in the arm and then say, "I was just kidding around"?

All of these "little" items add up to the whole person. If he is kind, considerate and patient, he will bring that into all areas of your marriage. These attitudes indicate how he will treat your children, your friends and family, and especially you. You don't need to sleep together to know if he will be a patient and considerate lover. Watch closely because the phonies are living a lie and cannot keep it up for long.

The biggest difference between marriage and living together is commitment. No matter what anyone says, living together outside of marriage is not a commitment. When you can walk out easily, you do not work hard at solving the very tough problems. If you marry, you must work hard to maintain the relationship. The man you have chosen will be the father of your children, your keeper if you are ill or disabled, the one who will still be there when the children move out to their own lives. Commitment means knowing this will happen. Living together will never provide that security.

Love, Dad

The Letter I Never Sent

Hey Kid,

This is the letter I never sent. I am going to include it in this book without you knowing because you may not let me if you saw it ahead of time.

When I read back over these letters, so many memories flash back into my mind. Some make me smile and others bring tears to my eyes. So much of our life together is in this book.

These letters make our relationship sound so perfect and you and I know it was not. I was far from a perfect man and I know many times you were frustrated or disappointed with me. These letters reflect not a perfect father, but one who is still trying to grow and pass on the best to his daughter.

The strongest emotion I feel when I read these letters is love. I know you and I are not big on verbalizing our feelings for each other. Each of us knows how much the other cares, but this time I want to say it: Dawn, I love you so very much.

Dad

About the Author

Alan Packer grew up in New Philadelphia, Ohio, and graduated from Greenville College in Illinois with a B.S. in Business. He served with the 101st Airborne in Vietnam in 1969. He was a roofing contractor for most of his life. He and his wife, Laura, now live in Blowing Rock, North Carolina.

To Order Additional Copies of "Hey Kid"

Write To:
Integrity House
P.O. Box 2108, Blowing Rock, NC 28605

Or Call:
1-800-915-1333

Each Book is $9.95 plus $2.00 Shipping
NC Residents Add 60¢ Sales Tax

HEY KID